KU-063-925

after work

after

work

This edition first published in the U.K. in 1999
by Hamlyn for WHSmith, Greenbridge Road,
Swindon SN3 3LD

Copyright © 1999 Octopus Publishing Group
Limited

Octopus Publishing Group Limited
2–4 Heron Quays
London E14 4JP

ISBN 0 600 59889 6

Printed in China

All rights reserved. No part of this publication
may be reproduced, stored in a retrieval
system or transmitted in any form or by any
means, electronic, mechanical, photocopying,
recording or otherwise, without the written
permission of the publisher.

Notes

1 Standard level spoon measurements are
used in all recipes.

1 tablespoon = one 15 ml spoon
1 teaspoon = one 5 ml spoon

2 Both imperial and metric measurements
have been given in all recipes. Use one set of
measurements only and not a mixture of both.

3 Measurements for canned food have been
given as a standard metric equivalent.

4 Eggs should be medium unless otherwise
stated. The Department of Health advises that
eggs should not be consumed raw. This book
may contain dishes made with lightly cooked
eggs. It is prudent for more vulnerable people,
such as pregnant and nursing mothers,
invalids, the elderly, babies and young
children, to avoid uncooked or lightly cooked
dishes made with eggs. Once prepared, these
dishes should be used immediately.

5 Milk should be full fat unless otherwise
stated.

6 Poultry should be cooked thoroughly. To
test if poultry is cooked, pierce the flesh
through the thickest part with a skewer or fork
– the juices should run clear, never pink or
red.

7 Fresh herbs should be used unless
otherwise stated. If unavailable, use dried
herbs as an alternative but halve the
quantities stated.

8 Pepper should be freshly ground black
pepper unless otherwise stated; season
according to taste.

9 Ovens should be preheated to the specified
temperature – if using a fan-assisted oven,
follow the manufacturer's instructions for
adjusting the time and the temperature.

10 Do not re-freeze a dish that has been
frozen previously.

11 This book includes dishes made with nuts
and nut derivatives. It is advisable for
customers with known allergic reactions to
nuts and nut derivatives and those who may
be potentially vulnerable to these allergies,
such as pregnant and nursing mothers,
invalids, the elderly, babies and children, to
avoid dishes made with nuts and nut oils.
It is also prudent to check the labels of pre-
prepared ingredients for the possible inclusion
of nut derivatives.

12 Vegetarians should look for the 'V' symbol
on a cheese to ensure it is made with
vegetarian rennet. There are vegetarian forms
of Parmesan, feta, Cheddar, Cheshire, red
Leicester, dolcelatte and many goats' cheeses,
among others.

introduction 6

light bites 10

Often, after a long day at work, the last thing you want to do is spend hours in the kitchen preparing dinner. You just want to collapse in front of the television with a glass of wine and a snack. WIth this in mind, here is a delicious collection of lighter meals, many of which can be prepared in advance with minimum effort.

international flavours 38

Add a little spice to your evenings with a selection of dishes from around the world. Ideal for informal entertaining or family meals and with a variety of pasta and stir-fry ideas included, these recipes are quick and easy to prepare as well.

quick fish dishes 54

Fish is a quick and healthy option for after work meals. It is extremely versatile and the recipes here demonstrate this. There are a number of ideas using a variety of ingredients, as well as marinades and sauces that will provide inspiration for any occasion.

meat & poultry for dinner 66

A popular choice for dinner, with plenty of scope both for quick recipes and those that require a little more time. There are many ideas here for a hungry family, as well as inspiration for special occasions.

sweet endings 82

What better way to finish the evening than with a delicious dessert? Whether you are looking for the finale to a fine meal or just fancy something sweet, this chapter will provide you with a selection of great ideas for the perfect dessert.

index 96

contents

6

introduction

After a long day at work or a day spent rushing around at home at a hectic pace, often the last thing we want to do is to have to prepare the evening meal. Quite often we have neither the energy nor the imagination to produce something that is both appetizing and quick. Increasingly, we turn instead to pre-packaged convenience foods, which require reheating in the microwave or oven and create little or even no washing up. While it might be a convenient lifestyle, it's certainly not a healthy one – with colourings, preservatives and additives galore – and it is also expensive. It is far better to create a home-made meal, using fresh ingredients if possible, which is where the recipes in this book come into their own.

Employ a little forward planning when shopping for the week, or simply stop off to buy one or two fresh ingredients on the way home from work. Team these with items from a well-stocked storecupboard of staples and you can easily create any of the dishes in this book. Some recipes require more preparation than others, yet none are difficult. All are ideal for a quick meal at the end of the day, whether you want something light or rather more filling, whether you fancy chicken, fish, meat or a vegetarian meal. You will find there is plenty of variety and choice here, and many of the recipes have been inspired by international cuisines.

The 'Light Bites' chapter includes soups, sandwiches and salads, while other chapters offer pasta dishes, stir-fries, quick fish dishes and various meat and poultry recipes. Not surprisingly, 'Sweet Endings' is the desserts chapter and provides such tempting dishes as baked bananas with rum cream, zabaglione and peaches brûlée among others, while the baking delights on offer include palmiers, cookies and chocolate brownies.

Fresh items for the shopping basket
Cheese is always a versatile ingredient and there is a huge choice of both traditional cheeses and newer varieties in the shops. To save you time in the kitchen, you can even buy it ready grated for use in sauces or pizza toppings or, in the case of Parmesan, in the form of shavings ready to top a steaming plate of lightly cooked vegetables or a hearty pasta dish. Cheddar has infinite uses – in sandwiches, baked potatoes and in sauces, on toast and on pizzas. Other cheeses are ideal with fruit or in salads, for example crumbled Roquefort or Stilton or thickly sliced mozzarella, which goes particularly well with tomatoes. A similar use can be found for feta cheese and for halloumi, both of which are also tasty when lightly grilled and served with fresh herbs and a drizzle of olive oil. Other versatile dairy products include soured cream, fromage frais and crème fraîche, all of which make ideal bases for salad dressings, for dips or for pasta sauces.

Fresh produce offers plenty of scope for imaginative quick cooking and should be used soon after purchase, in order to maximize the benefits of its nutrients and fresh flavour. Baby vegetables, as well as looking attractive, have the advantage of being more tender and of cooking more quickly than their older counterparts.

'Our life is frittered away by detail ... Simplify, simplify.'

Henry David Thoreau, *Walden*

Many are ideal in stir-fries, for example baby corn and courgettes. Others simply need light steaming or boiling before being served as a side dish. Packets of washed mixed salad leaves are invaluable time-savers, enabling you to produce both traditional and more exotic salads very quickly, or to supplement a main meal. Although it may be satisfying to prepare all of the ingredients yourself, it is undoubtedly time-consuming and the easy compromise between convenience foods and home cooking is to buy fresh vegetables, ready washed and sliced for instant use.

Mushrooms are important in many recipes. They come in many varieties, from open and closed cup mushrooms to the more exotic shiitake and oyster mushrooms, which are almost as easily available now. Fresh herbs are also easily obtainable, and many supermarkets sell them growing in pots.

Fresh pasta is very quick to cook, comes in all shapes and varieties and is always popular. Another staple is fresh bread, and there is a vast selection of breads from different regions of the world, such as ciabatta and focaccia from Italy, pitta breads and naan breads from the East – all of which can be plain or flavoured and are ideal accompaniments for salads, pasta dishes or curries, for example.

Storecupboard essentials

When it comes to keeping a well-stocked storecupboard, there are hundreds of ideas for ingredients to keep on standby. Jars of antipasto, sun-dried tomatoes and peppers, pesto and sun-dried tomato paste, among others, reflect the Mediterranean influence on much of our cooking these days, while red and green Thai curry pastes, coconut milk and hot chilli sauces are evidence of the impact of Indian, oriental and Caribbean cultures. The Chinese sauces such as soy and oyster are well known and have long been used in quick stir-fries and other oriental dishes.

Many dried herbs and spice mixtures are invaluable for adding flavour to a dish. Chilli and curry powder are particularly common and stock cubes and tomato purée are invaluable 'secret' ingredients, too. Ready-made mustard, English and French, is also a useful flavouring, as are balsamic vinegar and various oils for use in both salad dressings and for cooking.

Dried pastas, egg noodles and the numerous varieties of rice now available all come in handy and are substantial components of quick and easy cooking. Canned ingredients also have their uses, especially plum tomatoes; canned tuna, crab meat and shellfish are great in salads or pasta dishes, and canned beans are quicker alternatives to dried pulses, which require pre-soaking and boiling before use. The freezer is a modern addition to the storecupboard – consider keeping it stocked with frozen prawns and ready-to-use garlic bread, in order to make and supplement meals in a moment. Lastly, ready-made pizza bases are widely available and offer endless possibilities for toppings.

So, try the recipes in this book for yourself and you will find that home cooking is still an option in this modern busy age. The judicious use of a few fresh ingredients supplemented by trusty storecupboard essentials can enable you to create some truly nourishing meals – fast food with a difference!

reuben sandwich ●

croque monsieur ●

salami, mozzarella & pepper toasts ●

stuffed french bread ●

quick focaccia pizzas with pepperoni ●

pear & stilton salad ●

summer melon salad ●

tuscan nectarine & avocado salad ●

beetroot & pink grapefruit salad ●

rosy beetroot salad ●

two-tomato & mozzarella salad ●

salade niçoise ●

greek salad ●

hot potato salad ●

warm turkey salad ●

crab bisque ●

creamy tomato soup ●

carrot & ginger soup ●

mushroom soup ●

avocado & prawn mayo sandwiches ●

prawn & soft cheese pâté ●

light bites

12

2 slices of rye bread or firm wholemeal bread, 1 side toasted and buttered

1–2 thin slices of corned beef

sauerkraut to taste, well drained

slice of Swiss, Gruyère or Jarlsberg cheese

Russian Dressing:

250 g (8 oz) mayonnaise

1 tablespoon horseradish

4 teaspoons tomato chutney

1 very small onion, very finely chopped

To Garnish:

sliced gherkins

parsley sprigs

chopped chives

1 Assemble the sandwich in the given order of the ingredients, with the toasted side of the bread inside. Place under a preheated grill and cook until the cheese melts, turning once, or cook in an electric sandwich toaster.

2 To make the Russian dressing, put all the ingredients in a bowl and stir together until combined.

3 Garnish the sandwich with sliced gherkins, parsley sprigs and chives and serve with the dressing.

Serves 1	
Preparation time: 3 minutes	
Cooking time: 3 minutes	

reuben sandwich

1 Spread half the butter over 1 side of the bread only. Place a slice of Gruyère on 2 of the buttered slices, top with a slice of ham and season with a little black pepper. Top with the remaining slices of bread, buttered sides inwards, pressing down firmly.

2 Melt the remaining butter with the oil in a frying pan, and fry the croques until golden brown, turning once. Serve immediately.

50 g (2 oz) butter

4 slices of bread from a white sandwich loaf

2 slices of Gruyère cheese

2 thin slices of cooked lean ham

3 tablespoons sunflower oil

pepper

Serves 2

Preparation time: 5 minutes

Cooking time: 5 minutes

croque monsieur

salami, mozzarella & pepper toasts

4 thick slices of crusty farmhouse bread

125 g (4 oz) salami, rinded and thinly sliced

4 tomatoes, skinned (see below) and sliced

1 green or yellow pepper, cored, deseeded and sliced

75 g (3 oz) mozzarella cheese, thinly sliced

1 teaspoon dried mixed herbs

4–8 small black olives

salt and pepper

parsley sprigs, to garnish

Makes 4
Preparation time: 15 minutes
Cooking time: 11 minutes

1 Place the bread under a preheated hot grill and toast until golden on 1 side.

2 Turn the bread slices over and cover with the salami and tomatoes, adding salt and pepper to taste. Top with the slices of pepper and mozzarella. Sprinkle over the herbs, place under a preheated moderate grill and toast for about 10 minutes until cooked through and bubbling.

3 Serve hot, topped with the black olives and garnished with sprigs of parsley.

■ To skin tomatoes, slash the skin of each one once or twice with a sharp knife, place them in a bowl and pour over boiling water to cover. Leave to stand for 5 minutes, then drain and remove the skins which will have started to peel back around the slashes you have made.

stuffed french bread

1 To make the coleslaw, thoroughly mix together the cabbage, onion, carrot, celery, raisins and walnuts. Bind together with the mayonnaise.

2 Split the loaf in half horizontally. Spread the butter thinly on the inside of the loaf. Spread the coleslaw along the length of the bottom half of the loaf and top with the lettuce, mortadella, salami, smoked cheese, blue cheese, egg and tomato, arranged attractively.

3 Press the loaf halves firmly together and cut vertically into 3 thick sections to serve.

1 large long crusty French stick

25 g (1 oz) butter

2 lettuce leaves, shredded

3 slices of mortadella, rolled

25 g (1 oz) salami, rolled

50 g (2 oz) smoked cheese, sliced

50 g (2 oz) blue cheesé, sliced

1 hard-boiled egg, sliced

1 large beef tomato, sliced

Coleslaw:

125 g (4 oz) white cabbage, grated

25 g (1 oz) onion, grated

1 small carrot, grated

1 celery stick, chopped

15 g (½ oz) raisins

3 walnuts, coarsely chopped

3–4 tablespoons mayonnaise

Serves 3
Preparation time: 15 minutes

■ Mortadella is a large Italian pork sausage, containing garlic and other flavourings such as coriander seeds or pistachio nuts. It could be replaced in this recipe by any cooked or lightly smoked sausage.

quick focaccia pizzas with pepperoni

1 Combine the peppers, sun-dried tomatoes, half the Parmesan, the coriander or parsley, garlic and pepperoni in a bowl and season with salt and pepper.

2 Put the slices of focaccia or ciabatta bread on a greased baking sheet. Spread a little of the pepper mixture over each. Sprinkle with the remaining Parmesan and a few drops of olive oil.

3 Bake in a preheated oven, 240°C (475°F), Gas Mark 9, for 5–10 minutes, until the topping is bubbling. Serve immediately, garnished with basil leaves.

3 bottled roasted peppers, drained and diced

3 sun-dried tomatoes, preserved in oil, drained and diced

6 tablespoons freshly grated Parmesan cheese

3 tablespoons finely chopped fresh coriander or flat leaf parsley

2 garlic cloves, finely chopped

75 g (3 oz) pepperoni, chopped

12 slices of focaccia or ciabatta bread

olive oil, for sprinkling

salt and pepper

basil leaves, to garnish

Serves 4–6

Preparation time: 10 minutes

Cooking time: 5–10 minutes

1 Heat a griddle pan.

2 Cut each pear into quarters and remove the core, then slice each quarter in half. Place the slices of pear on the griddle and cook on each side for 1 minute. Remove and sprinkle them with the lemon juice.

3 Pile the spinach or lettuce on a large platter and arrange the pears on top. Sprinkle with the walnuts and crumbled Stilton and spoon over the walnut oil. Serve immediately.

4 pears

4 tablespoons lemon juice

250 g (8 oz) young spinach leaves or lettuce

4 walnuts, coarsely chopped

250 g (8 oz) Stilton, crumbled

4 tablespoons walnut oil

Serves 4

Preparation time: 10 minutes

Cooking time: 2 minutes

pear & stilton salad

summer melon salad

1 Cut the melon into quarters, then remove the seeds and skin. Scoop the flesh into balls with a melon baller or cut into cubes.

2 To serve, arrange the shredded lettuce on 4 individual plates or a large serving dish. Arrange the pieces of melon, strawberry and cucumber on top of the lettuce.

3 Mix the French dressing with the mint and salt and pepper to taste. Pour the dressing over the salad just before serving and sprinkle with the flaked almonds. This salad goes very well with a selection of hard and soft cheeses, or slices of ham.

1 small ripe melon

1 small crisp lettuce, shredded

125 g (4 oz) strawberries, hulled and thinly sliced

7 cm (3 inch) piece of cucumber, thinly sliced

4 tablespoons French dressing

2 tablespoons chopped mint

salt and pepper

15 g (½ oz) flaked almonds, to garnish

Serves 4

Preparation time: 15 minutes

■ If you like, present this salad as a starter in scooped-out melon shells. Use small ogen melons, allowing half a melon for each person. Using a sharp knife, cut the melons into a zigzag-shaped edge for a more decorative effect.

tuscan nectarine & avocado salad

1 Place the nectarine slices in a large salad bowl. Cut the avocado into small balls using a melon baller or teaspoon and add to the nectarines. Add the mixed salad leaves and tomatoes, tossing gently to blend, taking care not to break up the avocado balls.

2 To make the dressing, beat the oil and vinegar together until well blended and lightly thickened. Add the garlic, mustard, tarragon, chives and salt and pepper to taste, blending well. Spoon the dressing over the salad and toss lightly to mix. Serve at once with chunks of wholemeal or granary bread.

2 fresh nectarines, peeled and thinly sliced

1 avocado, halved and stoned

250 g (8 oz) mixed salad leaves (such as curly endive, lamb's lettuce, radicchio, chicory leaves)

8–12 small cherry tomatoes, halved

Dressing:

5 tablespoons olive oil

5 teaspoons tarragon vinegar

1 garlic clove, crushed

1 teaspoon wholegrain mustard

1 teaspoon chopped tarragon

1 teaspoon chopped chives

salt and pepper

Serves 4

Preparation time: 10 minutes

22

beetroot & pink grapefruit salad

1 Place the beetroot in a large salad bowl.

2 Cut a thin slice off the bottom of the grapefruit and place them, cut side down, on a board. Cut off the rind in strips, working from the top down. Take care to remove all the white pith. Holding the grapefruit over the salad bowl to catch any juice, cut out the segments with a knife. Add the segments to the bowl of beetroot, stir in the hazelnuts and toss lightly.

3 Whisk the raspberry vinegar, hazelnut oil and garlic in a small bowl then pour over the beetroot mixture. Add salt and pepper to taste and toss well. Arrange the radicchio and spinach leaves on individual plates and spoon over the beetroot, hazelnut and grapefruit mixture.

750 g (1½ lb) raw young beetroot, peeled and cut into fine julienne strips or finely grated

2 pink grapefruit

50 g (2 oz) shelled hazelnuts, roasted and coarsely chopped

1 tablespoon raspberry vinegar

3 tablespoons hazelnut oil

1 garlic clove, crushed

1 radicchio, leaves separated

250 g (8 oz) young spinach leaves

salt and pepper

Serves 4–6

Preparation time: 20 minutes

rosy
beetroot
salad

1   Place the diced beetroot and apricots in a shallow bowl.

2   To make the salad dressing, whisk all the ingredients together in a small bowl or shake them together in a screw-top jar until thoroughly combined.

3   To serve, pour the dressing over the beetroot mixture and toss lightly to mix. Finally, top with the shredded spring onions.

500 g (1 lb) cooked beetroot, cut into 1 cm (½ inch) dice

75 g (3 oz) ready-to-eat dried apricots, finely diced

2 spring onions, shredded

Dressing:

4 tablespoons olive or grapeseed oil

4 tablespoons red wine vinegar

1 teaspoon Dijon mustard

pinch of sugar

salt and pepper

Serves 4–6

Preparation time: 15 minutes

500 g (1 lb) fresh plum tomatoes, sliced

1 tablespoon chopped oregano

375 g (12 oz) mozzarella cheese, sliced

12 sun-dried tomatoes preserved in oil, drained and cut into strips

a few basil leaves

salt and pepper

Dressing:

5 tablespoons extra virgin olive oil

3 tablespoons oil from the sun-dried tomatoes

3 tablespoons red wine vinegar

½ garlic clove, crushed

pinch of sugar

Serves 4

Preparation time: 15 minutes

1 Arrange the plum tomato slices in a single layer on a large platter. Sprinkle with salt and pepper to taste, together with the oregano.

2 To make the dressing, whisk all the ingredients together in a small bowl or place in a screw-top jar, close the lid tightly and shake well to combine.

3 Arrange the slices of mozzarella on top of the sliced plum tomatoes and tuck the sun-dried tomato strips between them. Scatter the basil leaves over the top. Whisk or shake the dressing again, then pour over the salad and serve.

■ Made in various shapes, such as rounds and slabs, mozzarella is an Italian unripened curd cheese with a mild creamy taste. The best mozzarella is made from buffalo milk; however, the cow's milk version, which has a firmer texture, is often more commonly available.

two-tomato & mozzarella salad

salade
niçoise

1 Rub around the inside of a large salad bowl with the bruised garlic clove. Line the bowl with lettuce leaves. Chop the remaining lettuce leaves roughly and then arrange them in the bottom of the bowl.

2 Arrange the celery, cucumber, French beans, artichoke hearts quartered tomatoes, sliced pepper and onion, eggs, olives and anchovies on top of the lettuce leaves. Cut the tuna into chunks and place them in the bowl.

3 To make the dressing, mix together the olive oil and chopped basil with the seasoning. Pour the dressing over the salad and transfer to individual serving plates.

1 garlic clove, bruised

1 lettuce, leaves separated

125 g (4 oz) celery hearts, thinly sliced

125 g (4 oz) cucumber, peeled and thinly sliced

250 g (8 oz) small French beans, topped and tailed

250 g (8 oz) canned artichoke hearts, thinly sliced

500 g (1 lb) tomatoes, skinned (see page 15), quartered and deseeded

1 large green pepper, cored, deseeded and sliced

1 onion, sliced

4 hard-boiled eggs, halved

50 g (2 oz) black olives

8 canned anchovy fillets, drained

250 g (8 oz) can tuna in oil, drained

Dressing:

7 tablespoons olive oil

4 basil leaves, finely chopped

salt and pepper

Serves 4

Preparation time: 20 minutes

greek salad

1 Arrange the tomato slices, overlapping slightly, in concentric circles in a large serving bowl or on individual plates. Scatter the onion slices on top of the tomatoes.

2 Add the cucumber slices to the salad with the green pepper and black olives. Scatter the crumbled feta over the salad with the parsley. Season sparingly with salt (the amount required will depend on how salty the feta is) and grind a little black pepper over the top.

3 To make the dressing, whisk all the ingredients together in a small bowl or place in a screw-top jar, close the lid tightly and shake to combine. Pour over the salad and serve at once.

750 g (1½ lb) tomatoes, sliced

1 small onion, thinly sliced

1 small cucumber, peeled, halved lengthways and cut into slices

1 green pepper, cored, deseeded and thinly sliced

125 g (4 oz) black olives

250 g (8 oz) feta cheese, crumbled

flat leaf parsley leaves, roughly torn

salt and pepper

Dressing:

9 tablespoons extra virgin olive oil

3 tablespoons lemon juice

pinch of sugar

1 tablespoon chopped oregano

Serves 4–6

Preparation time: 20 minutes

hot potato salad

1 Place the potatoes in a saucepan of lightly salted boiling water and cook for 10–15 minutes until they are just tender. Drain. Cut the potatoes in half if large.

2 To make the caper vinaigrette, mix together the vinegar, mustard, capers and tarragon. Gradually whisk in the olive oil in a steady stream until amalgamated and season with salt and pepper.

3 Toss the warm potatoes with the vinaigrette, sprinkle with the crumbled feta and serve.

750 g (1½ lb) small red-skinned potatoes

125 g (4 oz) feta cheese, crumbled

Caper Vinaigrette:

1 tablespoon sherry vinegar

½ tablespoon Dijon mustard

2 tablespoons capers, drained and roughly chopped

1 tablespoon chopped tarragon

6 tablespoons extra virgin olive oil

salt and pepper

Serves 4
Preparation time: 10 minutes
Cooking time: 15 minutes

■ Capers are the green unopened buds of a Mediterranean shrub, and are used in their bottled, pickled form as a flavouring and garnish.

3 thick lemon grass stalks

25 g (1 oz) fresh root ginger, peeled and sliced

50 g (2 oz) butter

1 garlic clove

750 g (1½ lb) boneless, skinless turkey breast, cut into bite-sized cubes

1 tablespoon dark soy sauce

1 head of curly endive, leaves separated

3 spring onions, chopped

1 lemon, cut into wedges, to garnish

warm turkey salad

Serves 4

Preparation time: 15 minutes

Cooking time: 10 minutes

1 Cut the lemon grass in half lengthways then cut the strips in half widthways and mix them with the sliced ginger.

2 Melt the butter in a wok or large frying pan, crush the garlic into it and add the lemon grass and sliced ginger. Cook, stirring continuously, for 2 minutes, then add the pieces of turkey and continue stir-frying until the turkey has browned all over and is cooked through. Add the soy sauce to the turkey and cook gently for a few minutes more.

3 Arrange the endive leaves on a serving dish. Sprinkle the spring onions over the endive. Arrange the turkey on top and pour over any juices from the pan. Serve immediately, garnished with the lemon wedges. When served, the juice can be squeezed from these to add a little extra bite. Serve with a rice dish, boiled new potatoes or baked potatoes.

■ Lemon grass contains citrus oil and is used in oriental cooking for its wonderful lemony flavour and aroma. The long stalks are available in oriental stores and some supermarkets. Wrapped in newspaper, they will keep well for several weeks in the vegetable drawer of the refrigerator.

crab bisque

1 Combine the tomato soup and milk in a saucepan. Stir well over a moderate to high heat for 3 minutes. Add the crab meat with the brine, then stir in the curry powder, Worcestershire sauce and sherry. Cook for a further 3 minutes, or until the soup is almost boiling.

2 Remove the saucepan from the heat and stir in the cream. Serve the soup in heated soup bowls. Garnish each portion with chopped chives or parsley, if using. If the bisque is intended to be more substantial, serve it with croûtons.

300 g (10 oz) can condensed tomato soup

300 ml (½ pint) milk

175 g (6 oz) can white crab meat in brine

½ teaspoon mild curry powder

1 teaspoon Worcestershire sauce

2 teaspoons medium dry sherry

2 tablespoons double cream

finely chopped chives or parsley, to garnish (optional)

Serves 3–4

Preparation time: 5 minutes

Cooking time: 6 minutes

1 tablespoon sunflower oil

1 onion, chopped

1 garlic clove, crushed

400 g (13 oz) can chopped tomatoes

1 bay leaf or ½ dried bay leaf

450 ml (¾ pint) vegetable or chicken stock

1–2 teaspoons brown sugar

salt and pepper

single cream or natural yogurt, to garnish

creamy tomato soup

Serves 4
Preparation time: 10 minutes
Cooking time: 25 minutes

1 Heat the oil and cook the onion and garlic for 5 minutes. Add the canned tomatoes and their juice, salt and pepper, bay leaf and the stock. Bring to the boil, lower the heat and simmer for 10–15 minutes. Remove the bay leaf then purée the soup in a blender or food processor. Return to the pan and reheat with any extra seasoning required and the brown sugar. Serve garnished with the cream or yogurt.

■ Use 625 g (1¼ lb) fresh tomatoes instead of the canned when they are in season. You will obtain a better flavour and colour if you do not skin the tomatoes before cooking. Process them well in a blender or press through a sieve to remove all skin and pips.

2 tablespoons olive oil

1 large onion, chopped

1–2 garlic cloves, crushed

1 tablespoon finely grated fresh root ginger

375 g (12 oz) carrots, sliced

900 ml (1½ pints) vegetable or chicken stock

2 tablespoons fresh lime or lemon juice

salt and pepper

To Serve:

soured cream

2 spring onions, finely chopped

Serves 4
Preparation time: 15 minutes
Cooking time: 30 minutes

1 Heat the oil in a saucepan over a moderate heat, add the onion, garlic and ginger and cook gently for 5–6 minutes until softened.

2 Add the sliced carrots and stock. Bring to the boil then reduce the heat and simmer for 15–20 minutes until the carrots are tender.

3 Purée the soup in a liquidizer or food processor with the lime or lemon juice, in batches if necessary, until smooth. Strain the soup through a sieve and return to the saucepan to reheat.

4 Serve with a spoonful of soured cream in each bowl of soup and sprinkle with the chopped spring onions.

carrot & ginger soup

mushroom soup

1 Melt the butter in a large saucepan, add the mushrooms and stir over a moderate heat for 2–3 minutes, until the juices run. Put the lid on the pan and gently simmer the mushrooms in the juices for 5 minutes. Remove 2 tablespoons of the mushrooms and set aside to use as a garnish.

2 Stir the ground hazelnuts into the mushrooms in the pan, then add the stock, milk and nutmeg, and season to taste. Cover the pan and simmer gently for 10 minutes.

3 Purée the soup in a blender or food processor until smooth. Return to the rinsed out saucepan, stir in the cream and the reserved cooked mushrooms and reheat gently until hot but not boiling. Adjust the seasoning to taste and serve with crusty bread.

25 g (1 oz) butter

375 g (12 oz) closed cup mushrooms, sliced

25 g (1 oz) ground hazelnuts

600 ml (1 pint) vegetable or chicken stock

450 ml (¾ pint) milk

¼ teaspoon grated nutmeg

3 tablespoons single cream

salt and pepper

Serves 4

Preparation time: 10 minutes

Cooking time: 20 minutes

avocado & prawn mayo sandwiches

1 Spread the bread slices with the butter. Cut the avocado flesh into thin slices and toss in the lemon juice with salt and pepper to taste.

2 Mix the peeled prawns with the mayonnaise, a little cayenne pepper and salt to taste.

3 Arrange the avocado slices, prawns and a little lettuce on 4 of the slices, and top with the remaining bread slices.

8 slices of granary bread

50 g (2 oz) softened butter

1 ripe avocado, halved and stoned

4 tablespoons lemon juice

175 g (6 oz) cooked peeled prawns

4 tablespoons mayonnaise

cayenne pepper

lettuce leaves

salt and pepper

Makes 4

Preparation time: 10 minutes

prawn & soft cheese pâté

1 Beat the cheese in a mixing bowl with a wooden spoon until it is smooth. Add the chopped spring onion or shallot.

2 Stir the chopped prawns into the soft cheese mixture. Add the lemon juice, season well with salt and pepper, then add the dill or fennel. Mix well together.

3 Divide the mixture between 4 ramekins or small individual dishes. Smooth the tops. Garnish with prawns and dill or fennel fronds. Serve with toast or crusty bread.

175 g (6 oz) full-fat soft cheese

3 spring onions or 1 shallot, very finely chopped

250 g (8 oz) cooked peeled prawns, chopped

3 tablespoons lemon juice

1½ tablespoons finely chopped dill or fennel

salt and pepper

To Garnish:

whole cooked prawns

fronds of dill or fennel

Serves 4

Preparation time: 20 minutes

■ Shallots are mostly available in summer and autumn. They look like small onions but are milder tasting than the ordinary onion.

hot & sour thai noodles ●

chow mein ●

stir-fried turkey with pine nuts & green peppers ●

beef with mushrooms ●

stir-fried prawn supper ●

turkey & orange stir-fry ●

thai vegetable curry ●

vegetable frittata ●

quick pizza with ham & cheese ●

pasta with mixed seafood sauce ●

pasta with tuna & mushrooms ●

mediterranean spaghetti with ham ●

international
flavours

hot & sour
thai noodles

1   Heat the sunflower and sesame
oils in a small saucepan with the
garlic and chilli flakes until the oil starts
to smoke. Carefully strain the oil into a
wok or large frying pan.

2   Reheat the oil and when hot add
the carrots, broccoli, cauliflower,
mangetout and mushrooms. Stir-fry
for about 2 minutes, then add the
cabbage and bean sprouts and stir-fry
for a further 2 minutes until the
vegetables are just wilted. Remove
from the heat.

3   Meanwhile, soak the noodles
according to the packet
instructions. Whisk all the dressing
ingredients together in a small bowl
and season to taste. Drain the noodles
and toss with a little of the dressing.

4   Stir the remaining dressing into
the vegetables. Spoon the
noodles on to 4 individual plates, top
with the vegetables and cashew nuts
and serve at once. Alternatively,
arrange the noodles on a large plate,
top with the vegetables and leave to
cool for up to 1 hour. Sprinkle over the
nuts just before serving.

2 tablespoons sunflower oil

1 teaspoon sesame oil

2 garlic cloves, crushed

1 teaspoon chilli flakes

2 carrots, cut into matchsticks

50 g (2 oz) small broccoli florets

50 g (2 oz) small cauliflower florets

125 g (4 oz) mangetout, trimmed

125 g (4 oz) shiitake mushrooms,
sliced

125 g (4 oz) Chinese cabbage,
shredded

125 g (4 oz) bean sprouts

75 g (3 oz) rice vermicelli (noodles)

50 g (2 oz) cashew nuts

Dressing:

2½ tablespoons sunflower oil

1 tablespoon caster sugar

2 tablespoons lime juice

1 tablespoon rice or wine vinegar

1 tablespoon fish or light soy sauce

1 teaspoon Tabasco sauce

1 tablespoon chopped fresh
coriander

1 tablespoon chopped mint

salt and pepper

Serves 4

Preparation time: 15 minutes

Cooking time: 5 minutes

chow mein

1 Cook the noodles in a large saucepan of lightly salted boiling water for 3–5 minutes, or according to packet instructions. Drain and rinse under cold running water until cool. Set aside.

2 Heat a wok, then add about 3 tablespoons of the oil. When the oil is hot, add the onion, meat, mangetout or beans and the bean sprouts, and stir-fry for about 1 minute. Add salt to taste and stir a few more times, then remove the mixture from the wok with a slotted spoon and keep it hot.

3 Heat the remaining oil in the wok and add the spring onions and the noodles, together with about half the meat and vegetable mixture. Stir in the soy sauce, then stir-fry for 1–2 minutes, or until heated through.

4 Transfer the mixture from the wok to 4 warmed serving bowls, then arrange the remaining meat and vegetable mixture on top. Sprinkle with sesame oil or chilli sauce (or both, if preferred) and serve immediately.

500 g (1 lb) thin Chinese egg noodles

4 tablespoons vegetable oil

1 onion, finely sliced

125 g (4 oz) cooked pork, chicken or ham, thinly shredded

125 g (4 oz) mangetout or French beans, trimmed

125 g (4 oz) bean sprouts

2–3 spring onions, finely shredded

2 tablespoons light soy sauce

1 tablespoon sesame oil or chilli sauce

salt

Serves 4
Preparation time: 10 minutes
Cooking time: 8–10 minutes

■ Vegetarian Chow Mein can be made by preparing the ingredients as in the main recipe, substituting 1 finely sliced green pepper for the meat. Continue as in the main recipe, adding 175 g (6 oz) each of shredded Chinese cabbage leaves and whole baby spinach leaves to the wok 1–2 minutes before serving.

stir-fried turkey with pine nuts & green peppers

1 To make the sauce, blend the cornflour with the measured water, add the remaining sauce ingredients and set aside.

2 Heat 1 tablespoon of the oil in a wok, add the pine nuts and toss for 1–2 minutes until golden brown. Remove and drain on kitchen paper.

3 Gently stir-fry the onion, ginger and green peppers in the remaining oil for 3–4 minutes until softened but not coloured. Remove from the pan and set aside. Stir-fry the turkey pieces for 1–2 minutes until heated through.

4 Whisk the sauce, add to the wok and bring to the boil, stirring until it has thickened. Return the pepper mixture to the pan and toss to mix, then add the pine nuts and toss again. Season to taste and serve with Chinese egg noodles.

■ Pine nuts come from the Mediterranean stone pine. They have a high oil content, hence their tendency to go rancid, but can be kept in the refrigerator for up to 3 months.

3 tablespoons rapeseed oil

50 g (2 oz) pine nuts

1 onion, thinly sliced

2.5 cm (1 inch) piece of fresh root ginger, peeled and very thinly sliced

2 green peppers, cored, deseeded and cut into thin strips

500 g (1 lb) cooked turkey, cut diagonally into thin strips

salt and pepper

Sauce:

2 teaspoons cornflour

2 tablespoons water

2 tablespoons soy sauce

2 tablespoons rice wine or dry sherry

1 tablespoon wine vinegar

1 garlic clove, crushed

1 teaspoon soft dark brown sugar

Serves 4

Preparation time: 15 minutes

Cooking time: 10–15 minutes

beef with mushrooms

1 Soak the dried mushrooms in boiling water for 20 minutes. Drain, squeezing out the excess liquid, remove any tough stems and thinly slice the caps.

2 Heat the oil in a wok. Add the garlic and stir-fry until golden. Add the steak, ginger, black bean sauce, pepper and sugar. Cook, stirring constantly, until the steak is lightly browned. Stir in the mushrooms, chopped spring onions and chicken stock, and cook for 5 minutes.

3 Garnish with strips of spring onion and serve immediately with boiled rice.

125 g (4 oz) dried jelly mushrooms, black fungus (cloud ears) or shiitake mushrooms

2 tablespoons vegetable oil

1 garlic clove, crushed

125 g (4 oz) rump steak, finely sliced

2 tablespoons finely chopped fresh root ginger

1 tablespoon black bean sauce

¼ teaspoon pepper

1 teaspoon sugar

4 spring onions, chopped

125 ml (4 fl oz) chicken stock

2 spring onions, sliced into strips, to garnish

Serves 4

Preparation time: 10 minutes, plus soaking

Cooking time: 10 minutes

■ Dried mushrooms, available from oriental stores and some supermarkets, are a useful standby ingredient and keep for over a year. They require soaking in warm water before use to rehydrate them. Roughly 75 g (3 oz) of dried mushrooms are equal, when reconstituted, to 500 g (1 lb) fresh mushrooms.

stir-fried prawn supper

1 Heat the oil in a wok or deep frying pan, add the ginger and garlic and stir-fry over a moderate heat for 30 seconds. Add the spring onions, carrot and celery and stir-fry for 1 minute, then add the cauliflower and stir-fry for 30 seconds. Add the red and green peppers and stir-fry for a further 30 seconds. Add the prawns and cook for 2–3 minutes.

2 Mix together all the ingredients for the glaze in a bowl, pour into the pan and stir over a brisk heat until all the prawns and vegetables are coated. Turn on to warmed plates, garnish with the celery leaves and serve at once.

4 tablespoons vegetable oil

15 g (½ oz) fresh root ginger, peeled and finely sliced into matchsticks

2 garlic cloves, chopped

8 spring onions, diagonally sliced

1 carrot, cut into matchsticks

8 celery sticks, diagonally sliced

375 g (12 oz) cauliflower, separated into tiny florets

2 red peppers, cored, deseeded and thinly sliced

1 green pepper, cored, deseeded and thinly sliced

1 kg (2 lb) large raw peeled prawns

celery leaves, to garnish

Glaze:

2 teaspoons cornflour

6 tablespoons water

2 tablespoons white wine vinegar

2 teaspoons soy sauce

2 teaspoons tomato purée

salt and pepper

Serves 4

Preparation time: 20 minutes

Cooking time: 6–8 minutes

turkey & orange stir-fry

1 Remove the skin from the turkey if preferred. Cut the turkey into 3.5 cm (1½ inch) long strips, about 1 cm (½ inch) in width and thickness. Combine the soy sauce and orange juice in a shallow dish. Place the turkey portions in this marinade and leave for 30 minutes.

2 Grate the rind from the oranges and squeeze out the juice. Pour the orange juice into a measuring jug and add sufficient water to make it up to 150 ml (¼ pint). Blend the cornflour with this liquid and add a little salt and pepper. Remove the turkey from the marinade and drain well. Reserve the marinade.

3 Heat the two oils in a wok or heavy frying pan. Add the turkey and stir-fry for 4–5 minutes, then add the grated orange rind, peppers, celery and carrots. Continue stir-frying for a further 3 minutes. Pour in the cornflour and orange juice mixture, together with any leftover marinade. Stir as the liquid comes to the boil and thickens slightly. Serve immediately with cooked rice.

375 g (12 oz) turkey breast portions, thawed if frozen

1 tablespoon soy sauce

2 tablespoons orange juice

2 oranges

1 teaspoon cornflour

1 tablespoon sunflower oil

1 teaspoon sesame seed oil

½ red pepper, cored, deseeded and cut into strips

½ green pepper, cored, deseeded and cut into strips

3 celery sticks, diced

125 g (4 oz) carrots, cut into matchsticks

salt and pepper

Serves 4

Preparation time: 10 minutes, plus marinating

Cooking time: 10–12 minutes

thai vegetable curry

1 Place the ingredients for the fragrant water in a saucepan and boil for 1 minute. Remove from the heat and set aside for the flavour to infuse.

2 Place the ingredients for the green purée in a blender or food processor and process until smooth, adding a little water if necessary.

3 Heat the oil in a large frying pan or wok and stir-fry the green purée for 5–6 minutes. Pour the fragrant water through a strainer into the pan and add the puréed anchovies and the coconut mixed with a little water to a runny paste. Combine well to give a smooth mixture. Add the water chestnuts, baby sweetcorn cobs and bamboo shoots. (If you are using canned vegetables, use some of their liquid for stock – enough to make the curry runny but not watery.) Simmer the vegetables for 5–6 minutes. To serve, garnish with lime wedges and sprigs of basil.

4 tablespoons vegetable oil

2 anchovies, puréed

2 tablespoons desiccated coconut

175 g (6 oz) can water chestnuts

475 g (15 oz) baby sweetcorn cobs

175 g (6 oz) bamboo shoots, sliced

Fragrant Water:

175 ml (6 fl oz) water

4 tablespoons thinly pared lemon rind

Green Purée:

1 green pepper, chopped

1–6 green chillies

1 bunch of watercress

2 tablespoons chopped fresh coriander

4 spinach leaves

2–4 garlic cloves

5 cm (2 inch) piece of fresh root ginger, chopped

To Garnish:

lime wedges

basil sprigs

Serves 4	
Preparation time: 10 minutes	
Cooking time: 15 minutes	

vegetable frittata

1 Heat the olive oil in a large, heavy-based frying pan. Add the sliced onions and sauté very gently for 8–10 minutes until really soft, golden brown and almost caramelized. Add the courgettes and continue cooking until golden on both sides, stirring from time to time. Add the tomatoes and cook over a moderate heat until the mixture is thick.

2 Break the eggs into a large bowl and add the seasoning, grated Parmesan, torn basil and parsley. Beat well with a wire whisk until all the ingredients are thoroughly blended.

3 Drain off and discard any excess oil from the cooked tomato mixture. Add the mixture to the beaten eggs and stir together gently until they are well mixed.

4 Heat the butter in a large clean frying pan until it is hot and sizzling. Pour in the egg mixture and reduce the heat to a bare simmer – as low as it will go. Cook very gently until the omelette is firm and set underneath. Place under a preheated hot grill for a few seconds to set and brown the top. Slide out on to a plate and serve at room temperature cut into wedges.

3 tablespoons olive oil

2 onions, very finely sliced

3 courgettes, finely sliced

3 tomatoes, skinned (see page 15) and chopped

6 large eggs

50 g (2 oz) Parmesan cheese, freshly grated

few basil leaves, torn

1 tablespoon chopped parsley

25 g (1 oz) butter

salt and pepper

Serves 4

Preparation time: 25 minutes

Cooking time: 15–20 minutes

quick pizza with ham & cheese

1 Place the flours, any grains left in the sieve, a pinch of salt and the baking powder in a bowl. Mix together the oil and milk. Stir the liquid into the flour to make a firm dough. Roll it out on a floured surface to give a 25 cm (10 inch) round. Lift the dough on to a baking sheet and pinch the edges up slightly to form a lip to hold the filling.

2 Mix together the relish and Worcestershire sauce and spread evenly over the base. Arrange the onion, pepper, tomatoes and ham on top and scatter over the grated mozzarella. Sprinkle with oregano and black pepper. Bake in a preheated oven, 200°C (400°F), Gas Mark 6, for 25–30 minutes until golden. Serve with a green salad.

125 g (4 oz) white self-raising flour, sifted

150 g (5 oz) granary flour, sifted

1 teaspoon baking powder

50 ml (2 fl oz) olive or soya oil

150 ml (¼ pint) semi-skimmed milk

6 tablespoons tomato relish

1 teaspoon Worcestershire sauce

1 small onion, thinly sliced

1 small green pepper, cored, deseeded and thinly sliced

4 tomatoes, sliced

125 g (4 oz) cooked lean ham, cut into thin strips

125 g (4 oz) mozzarella cheese, grated

1 tablespoon chopped oregano

salt and pepper

Serves 3–4
Preparation time: 20 minutes
Cooking time: 25–30 minutes

1. Add a dash of oil and a generous pinch of salt to a large saucepan of boiling water. Add the pasta and cook for 8–12 minutes, or according to packet instructions, until tender. Drain thoroughly and keep warm until the sauce is ready.

2. While the pasta is cooking, melt the butter in a saucepan. Add the onion and garlic and gently fry for 2 minutes. Stir in the flour and cook for 1 minute. Gradually add the stock and wine, stirring constantly. Bring to the boil.

3. Reduce the heat and stir in the monkfish and scallops. Cook gently for 2–3 minutes. Stir in the crab meat, prawns and flat leaf parsley. Season with salt and pepper and heat gently for 1 minute. Add the cream and gently heat through.

4. Toss the pasta with half the sauce. Transfer to a warmed serving dish. Spoon the remaining sauce over the top of the pasta and serve immediately.

dash of oil

500 g (1 lb) pasta shells (conchiglie)

50 g (2 oz) butter

1 onion, finely chopped

1 garlic clove, crushed

50 g (2 oz) plain flour

500 ml (17 fl oz) vegetable stock

150 ml (¼ pint) white wine

125 g (4 oz) monkfish, cubed

6 scallops, quartered

50 g (2 oz) canned or thawed frozen crab meat

125 g (4 oz) cooked peeled prawns

1 tablespoon chopped flat leaf parsley

150 ml (¼ pint) single cream

salt and pepper

Serves 4–6

Preparation time: 15 minutes

Cooking time: 20 minutes

---

pasta with mixed seafood sauce

pasta with tuna & mushrooms

1 Add a dash of oil and a generous pinch of salt to a large saucepan of boiling water. Add the penne or macaroni and cook for 8–12 minutes, or according to packet instructions, until tender.

2 Meanwhile, heat the olive oil in a saucepan, add the garlic, mushrooms and red pepper and fry gently for 3 minutes, until the vegetables are tender but still firm.

3 Flake the tuna but do not drain. Add to the pan and stir gently until the sauce is blended and heated through. Season the sauce to taste with salt and pepper.

4 Drain the cooked pasta and toss with half of the sauce. Transfer to a warmed serving dish or warmed individual plates and spoon the remaining sauce over the top. Garnish with chopped parsley or basil and serve immediately.

125 ml (4 fl oz) olive oil, plus a dash extra

500 g (1 lb) pasta quills (penne) or macaroni

1 garlic clove, crushed

250 g (8 oz) mushrooms, finely sliced

1 small red pepper, cored, deseeded and thinly sliced

200 g (7 oz) can tuna in oil

salt and pepper

finely chopped parsley or basil, to garnish

Serves 4–6

Preparation time: 10 minutes

Cooking time: 12 minutes

mediterranean spaghetti with ham

1 Cook the pasta in a large saucepan of lightly salted boiling water until tender – about 12 minutes. Add 1 tablespoon of the oil to the water to prevent the pasta sticking together.

2 Meanwhile, heat the remaining oil in a saucepan over a moderate heat. Add the garlic and tomatoes and cook, stirring, for 5 minutes. Add the ham to the pan with the chopped basil. Season with salt and pepper to taste. Cover the pan and simmer very gently for 10 minutes. Add the olives and capers.

3 Drain the pasta thoroughly and toss it in the sauce. Transfer to a warmed deep serving dish and garnish with sprigs of basil. Serve immediately, with grated Parmesan for sprinkling.

375 g (12 oz) dried spaghetti or tagliatelle

2 tablespoons olive oil

1 garlic clove, crushed

750 g (1½ lb) ripe tomatoes, skinned (see page 15) and chopped

375 g (12 oz) cooked lean ham, trimmed of fat and cut into thin strips

2 tablespoons chopped basil leaves

50 g (2 oz) black olives, pitted and roughly chopped

2 tablespoons capers (see page 28)

salt and pepper

basil sprigs, to garnish

freshly grated Parmesan cheese, to serve

Serves 6
Preparation time: 20 minutes
Cooking time: 16 minutes

cod steaks à la grecque ●

cod kebabs with barbecue sauce ●

spinach & cod omelette ●

fishy baked spuds ●

spicy haddock fritters ●

spicy fried fishcakes ●

prawn chilli fry ●

fish casserole with peppers ●

salmon steaks in red wine ●

quick fish dishes

cod steaks à la grecque

1 Gently cook the onion and garlic in a pan in a little olive oil until transparent, but do not let them brown. Add the tomato purée, fish stock, green and black olives and sherry and season with salt and pepper to taste.

2 Arrange the cod steaks in a lightly greased ovenproof dish, and pour the sauce over and around them. Bake in a preheated oven, 180°C (350°F), Gas Mark 4, for 20–25 minutes.

3 Garnish the steaks with fennel sprigs and celery leaves and serve immediately with a selection of green vegetables.

1 onion, finely chopped

1 garlic clove, crushed

a little olive oil

50 g (2 oz) tomato purée

150 ml (¼ pint) fish stock

6 green and 6 black olives, pitted

2 tablespoons dry sherry

4 cod steaks

salt and pepper

To Garnish:

fennel sprigs

celery leaves

Serves 4
Preparation time: 10 minutes
Cooking time: 30–35 minutes

■ Ready-made fish stock is available from well-stocked supermarkets.

cod kebabs with barbecue sauce

1 Place the pieces of cod in a glass or earthenware dish. Combine the marinade ingredients, pour over the cod and leave to marinate for 20 minutes, turning occasionally.

2 Oil 4 kebab skewers and thread on the pieces of cod, interspersed with the rosemary sprigs and mushrooms.

3 Place the kebabs under a preheated grill for about 5 minutes, turning and basting with the marinade. Serve immediately with a crisp green salad, and pour the remaining marinade over the kebabs.

750 g (1½ lb) cod steaks, skinned, boned and cut into cubes

12 rosemary sprigs

12–16 button mushrooms, wiped and stalks removed

Marinade:

2 teaspoons prepared mustard

4 teaspoons Worcestershire sauce

4 tablespoons red wine vinegar

4 tablespoons olive or sunflower oil

4 tablespoons tomato ketchup

Serves 4

Preparation time: 15 minutes, plus marinating

Cooking time: 5 minutes

58

spinach
& cod
omelette

1 Beat the eggs and yogurt together in a bowl, then add the chopped parsley and season with pepper to taste.

2 Melt the butter in a large omelette pan and cook the onion or shallot until pale and soft. Add the chopped spinach and stir for about 1 minute, until the leaves soften. Add the pieces of fish. Pour in the beaten egg mixture and cook until the omelette is set. Finish by browning under the grill.

3 Slide the unfolded omelette on to a warmed serving plate and serve immediately.

6 eggs

4 tablespoons unsweetened natural yogurt

1 tablespoon chopped parsley

25 g (1 oz) butter

1 small onion or shallot, finely chopped

12 spinach leaves, finely chopped

175 g (6 oz) cooked cod fillets, skinned and cut into cubes

75 g (3 oz) cooked smoked fish fillets (such as kipper or mackerel), skinned and cut into cubes

pepper

Serves 2

Preparation time: 15 minutes

Cooking time: 15 minutes

fishy baked spuds

1   Bake the potatoes in a preheated oven, 200°C (400°F), Gas Mark 6, for about 1 hour or, alternatively, bake them at full power in the microwave for about 20 minutes.

2   To make the cottage cheese filling, first sauté the sunflower seeds in a frying pan containing a little oil. Mix together the cooked cod, kipper and cottage cheese, season to taste with salt and pepper and use to fill the cooked potatoes. Garnish the potatoes with the sunflower seeds and chopped parsley.

3   Alternatively, to make the prawn and spring onion filling, combine the prawns, soured cream, yogurt and a few drops of Tabasco sauce in a bowl with 4 of the chopped spring onions. Season to taste and use to fill the cooked potatoes. Garnish with the remaining chopped spring onion.

4   When the potatoes are cooked, remove from the oven and cut them almost in half lengthways and crossways to form a criss-cross in the centre of the potato. Then heap your chosen filling in the centre of the potatoes and serve alone or with a selection of salads.

4 baking potatoes

Cottage Cheese, Cod & Kipper Filling:

2 tablespoons sunflower seeds

a little oil

125 g (4 oz) cooked cod, flaked

125 g (4 oz) cooked kipper fillet, skinned and cut into thin strips

250 g (8 oz) cottage cheese

salt and pepper

2 tablespoons chopped parsley, to garnish

Prawn & Spring Onion Filling:

250 g (8 oz) cooked peeled prawns

150 ml (¼ pint) soured cream

150 ml (¼ pint) unsweetened natural yogurt

a few drops of Tabasco sauce

5 spring onions, finely chopped

salt and pepper

Serves 4

Preparation time: 10 minutes

Cooking time: 1 hour

spicy haddock fritters

1 Whisk the egg until frothy, then beat in the measured water. Mix well until amalgamated, then gradually sift in the flour, whisking all the time to make a really smooth batter. Add the curry powder and salt and pepper to taste and beat again.

2 Fill a deep-fryer one-third full with oil and heat to a temperature of 190°C (375°F), or until a cube of stale bread turns golden in 30 seconds.

3 Pat the fish cubes dry with kitchen paper then add to the bowl of batter, turning them to coat completely. Lower a few cubes into the hot oil and deep-fry for 4–5 minutes or until golden and puffed. Lift out with a slotted spoon and drain on kitchen paper. Keep hot while frying the remaining fritters.

4 Mix together the mayonnaise, yogurt, turmeric and chilli and put into a small bowl. Serve with the fritters, garnished with coriander leaves and lemon slices.

1 large egg

300 ml (½ pint) water

250 g (8 oz) plain flour

1–2 teaspoons curry powder

oil, for deep-frying

1 kg (2 lb) haddock fillet, skinned, cut into bite-sized cubes

175 ml (6 fl oz) thick mayonnaise

3 tablespoons unsweetened natural yogurt

¼ teaspoon ground turmeric

1 small green chilli, deseeded and very finely chopped

salt and pepper

To Garnish:

lemon slices

fresh coriander leaves

Serves 4	
Preparation time: 15–20 minutes	
Cooking time: 15–20 minutes	

spicy fried fishcakes

1 Combine the fish and the curry paste in a blender or food processor, and process until the fish is finely chopped. Alternatively, use a pestle and mortar.

2 Transfer the fish mixture to a bowl and add the egg and fish sauce. Knead to make a stiff mixture then work in the French beans.

3 Form the mixture into 16–20 balls and flatten each one to a round about 1 cm (½ inch) thick. Heat the oil in a large frying pan, add the fishcakes and fry for 4–5 minutes on each side over a medium heat. Do not allow the fishcakes to overcook, or they will dry out.

4 Lift the fishcakes out of the pan with a slotted spoon and drain on kitchen paper. Transfer to a serving plate and serve hot with a salad.

500 g (1 lb) cod fillet, skinned and cut into cubes

3 tablespoons red Thai curry paste

1 egg

3 tablespoons fish sauce (nam pla)

75 g (3 oz) French beans, finely chopped

oil, for shallow-frying

Serves 4
Preparation time: 15 minutes
Cooking time: 10 minutes

■ Thai curry paste is available red or green, and combines the classic Thai flavours of lemon grass, galangal, shrimp paste, shallots and garlic. Another well-known Thai ingredient is nam pla, a fish sauce made from fermented fish or seafood with a distinctive slightly salty flavour. It is available in bottles from supermarkets and oriental stores.

prawn chilli fry

1 Heat the oil in a large frying pan, add the onions and fry gently for 5 minutes until soft and golden. Add the chillies, ginger, chilli powder, turmeric and salt to taste and fry, stirring, for 2 minutes.

2 Add the peeled prawns and cook, uncovered, for about 3 minutes, or until all the moisture has evaporated. Serve immediately with boiled or fried rice, if liked.

■ Chillies vary in colour from yellow and green to red and black and from mildly warm to blisteringly hot. The seeds are the hottest part so discard them if you want a mild chilli flavour. Take care when preparing chillies; wash your hands, knives and chopping board thoroughly and never let any part of the chilli go near your eyes.

3 tablespoons oil

3 onions, sliced

2 green chillies, chopped

2.5 cm (1 inch) piece of fresh root ginger, peeled and chopped

½ teaspoon chilli powder

½ teaspoon turmeric

375 g (12 oz) cooked tiger prawns

salt

Serves 4

Preparation time: 5–10 minutes

Cooking time: 10 minutes

fish casserole with peppers

1 Heat the oil in a flameproof casserole. Add the spring onions, and fry for about 1 minute, stirring, without browning. Add the peppers and stir-fry for about 3 minutes.

2 Add the tomatoes with their juice and the sugar and bring to the boil. Simmer for 5 minutes, then put the cod on top. Sprinkle over the lemon juice, season with pepper to taste and sprinkle with the parsley.

3 Cover and cook in a preheated oven, 180°C (350°F), Gas Mark 4, for 15–20 minutes, depending on the thickness of the fillets.

4 Serve each portion of fish with some of the pepper mixture and accompany with wholemeal rolls.

1 tablespoon oil

3 spring onions, chopped, including green part

1 green pepper, cored, deseeded and cut into strips

1 red pepper, cored, deseeded and cut into strips

400 g (13 oz) can chopped tomatoes

½ teaspoon sugar

4–6 frozen cod fillets, thawed

4 tablespoons lemon juice

1 heaped teaspoon chopped parsley

pepper

Serves 4–6
Preparation time: 10 minutes
Cooking time: 30–35 minutes

1 Rinse the salmon steaks quickly in cold water, then pat dry.

2 Melt 50 g (2 oz) of the butter in a large flameproof dish into which the salmon will fit snugly. Add the shallots and sweat for 2 minutes. Put the salmon steaks in the dish and brown for 1 minute on each side over a high heat.

3 Sprinkle over the remaining ingredients, cover with buttered greaseproof paper and cook in a preheated oven, 190°C (375°F), Gas Mark 5, for 10–15 minutes until the salmon steaks are just done.

4 Pour the cooking juices into a small saucepan; keep the salmon warm. Cut the rest of the butter into small pieces and whisk into the pan, one at a time, beating until each piece is absorbed. Stop when the sauce is smooth and glossy. Pour immediately over the salmon, garnish with parsley and serve with a selection of vegetables.

6 salmon steaks, about 2.5 cm (1 inch) thick

125–150 g (4–5 oz) unsalted butter

6 shallots, finely chopped

small bunch of parsley, finely chopped

1 garlic clove, finely chopped

6 black peppercorns, crushed

300 ml (½ pint) red wine

salt

parsley sprigs, to garnish

Serves 6

Preparation time: 10 minutes

Cooking time: 20–25 minutes

salmon steaks in red wine

beef kebabs with horseradish salsa •
beef & mushroon burgers •
lamb with cranberries & honey •
apple & stilton pork •
pork chops with cider •
green pepper steak •
steak au poivre •
chilli con carne •
sausage waffles •
chicken schnitzels •
citrus chicken •
duck breasts with spicy mango relish •

meat & poultry for dinner

750 g (1½ lb) piece of sirloin steak, trimmed and cut into 16 long thin strips

8 long rosemary sprigs

4 tablespoons balsamic vinegar

175 ml (6 fl oz) red wine

4 tablespoons olive oil

1 tablespoon cracked black pepper

salt

Horseradish Salsa:

250 g (8 oz) cooked beetroot, peeled and chopped

½ red onion, finely chopped

1–2 tablespoons finely grated fresh horseradish or horseradish relish, or to taste

1 Thread 2 pieces of steak on to each sprig of rosemary concertina fashion and place in a shallow dish. Mix together the vinegar, red wine, olive oil and pepper and pour over the steak. Turn to coat thoroughly, then cover and leave to marinate for 1–2 hours.

2 To make the horseradish salsa, mix together the beetroot, onion and horseradish in a bowl, season and set aside.

3 Remove the kebabs from the marinade, sprinkle with a little salt and place on an oiled rack under a preheated grill and cook for 3–4 minutes on each side, basting frequently with the remaining marinade. Serve with the salsa.

Serves 4

Preparation time: 20 minutes, plus marinating

Cooking time: 6–8 minutes

beef kebabs with horseradish salsa

beef & mushroom burgers

1 Mix together the minced beef, onion, mushrooms and breadcrumbs in a bowl. Stir in the lemon rind and add the beaten egg to bind the mixture. Season lightly with salt and pepper.

2 Dust your hands with the flour and form the beef and mushroom mixture into 12 flat burgers. Place them under a preheated hot grill and cook for 8–10 minutes, turning once, until they are lightly browned and cooked through.

3 To serve, split open the warm buns and place the burgers inside with the shredded lettuce and sliced tomatoes.

500 g (1 lb) lean minced beef

1 small onion, finely chopped

125 g (4 oz) open cup mushrooms, finely chopped

125 g (4 oz) fresh wholemeal breadcrumbs

finely grated rind of ½ lemon

1 egg, beaten

2 tablespoons wholemeal flour

salt and pepper

To Serve:

12 wholemeal buns, warmed

1 lettuce, shredded

4 firm tomatoes, sliced

Serves 6
Preparation time: 15 minutes
Cooking time: 8–10 minutes

lamb with cranberries & honey

1 Trim any visible fat from the lamb and place in a large dish. Pour over the cranberry juice. Cover and leave to marinate for at least 4 hours or overnight. Drain the meat, reserving the marinade.

2 Place the lamb under a preheated hot grill and cook for 7–10 minutes, or until the lamb is cooked to your liking, turning once.

3 Meanwhile, place the marinade in a saucepan with the cranberries and boil rapidly for 5 minutes, or until the cranberries are soft. Add the honey and stir until it has melted.

4 Serve the lamb with the cranberry sauce spooned over the top and garnished with sprigs of mint.

4 lean lamb chops or leg steaks

150 ml (¼ pint) cranberry juice

125 g (4 oz) fresh or frozen cranberries

3 tablespoons clear honey

mint sprigs, to garnish

Serves 4

Preparation time: 10 minutes, plus marinating

Cooking time: 7–10 minutes

apple & stilton pork

1 Melt the butter in a frying pan, add the pork steaks and fry over a moderate heat for 15–20 minutes, turning once, until cooked through. Transfer to an ovenproof serving dish and keep warm.

2 Place the grated Stilton in a small mixing bowl. Core and finely chop half the apple, leaving the skin on, and add to the cheese with 2 tablespoons of the wine and 1 tablespoon of the cream. Spoon the mixture over the pork steaks and place under a hot grill until the topping is bubbling and golden brown.

3 Meanwhile, slice the remaining apple thinly and add to the frying pan with the remaining wine. Season with salt and pepper and simmer gently for 2–3 minutes until the apple slices are tender. Stir in the remaining cream and bring to the boil.

4 Place the pork steaks on warmed serving plates and pour the sauce over the top. Sprinkle with the parsley and serve immediately.

15 g (½ oz) butter

2 boneless pork steaks, about 175 g (6 oz) each

50 g (2 oz) Stilton cheese, grated

1 red dessert apple

5 tablespoons dry white wine

5 tablespoons double cream

salt and pepper

2 teaspoons chopped parsley, to garnish

Serves 2

Preparation time: 15 minutes

Cooking time: 20–25 minutes

■ Use 50 g (2 oz) freshly grated Parmesan or mature Cheddar instead of the Stilton, if preferred.

1 Mix the chopped shallots or small onions and parsley together in a bowl, with salt and pepper to taste. Score the pork chops on both sides and spread with the mixture. Spoon over a little melted butter. Cook under a preheated moderate grill for about 15 minutes on each side, until tender.

2 Transfer the chops to a frying pan. Drain any excess fat from the grill pan and pour the juices over the chops. Add the cider and boil for 2 minutes until the liquid has reduced. Stir in the Calvados, if using.

3 Transfer the chops to a warmed serving dish and garnish with sage leaves.

4 shallots or small onions, chopped

2 tablespoons chopped parsley

4 pork chops, about 150 g (5 oz) each

25 g (1 oz) butter, melted

150 ml (¼ pint) dry cider

1 tablespoon Calvados (optional)

salt and pepper

sage leaves, to garnish

Serves 4
Preparation time: 10 minutes
Cooking time: 35 minutes

pork chops with cider

green pepper steak

1 Season the steaks with salt and press the peppercorns and thyme into the meat. Place the steaks under a preheated hot grill and cook for 2–3 minutes on each side until browned, or until cooked according to taste.

2 Meanwhile, put the garlic, mushrooms and wine in a saucepan and bring to the boil. Boil rapidly until reduced and thickened, then stir in the Worcestershire sauce, mustard and spring onions.

3 Arrange the steaks on warmed serving plates and spoon over the sauce. Garnish with thyme and serve immediately with a green salad or vegetable.

■ Green peppercorns are the soft unripe version of the familiar hard black peppercorn. They are usually sold in brine, and are considerably milder than black peppercorns.

2 x 150 g (5 oz) sirloin or fillet steaks

2 tablespoons green peppercorns

1 tablespoon chopped thyme

1 garlic clove, crushed

50 g (2 oz) button mushrooms, sliced

125 ml (4 fl oz) dry red wine

dash of Worcestershire sauce

1 teaspoon French mustard

2 spring onions, chopped

salt

thyme sprigs, to garnish

Serves 2

Preparation time: 5 minutes

Cooking time: 8 minutes

steak au poivre

1 Crush half the peppercorns and rub into the steaks. Season to taste with salt. Melt the butter in a large frying pan, add the steaks and fry quickly on both sides until browned. Then cook for 3–5 minutes on each side, according to taste. Pour over the brandy, remove the pan from the heat and ignite. When the flames have died down, arrange the steaks on a warmed serving plate.

2 Add the cream to the pan and cook, without boiling, for 1 minute. Add the remaining peppercorns to the pan. Spoon over the steaks, garnish with watercress and serve immediately.

2 tablespoons green peppercorns, or 1 tablespoon black peppercorns

4 x 150 g (5 oz) rump or fillet steaks

50 g (2 oz) butter

2 tablespoons brandy

150 ml (5 fl oz) double cream

salt

watercress sprigs, to garnish

Serves 4
Preparation time: 5 minutes
Cooking time: 10–15 minutes

chilli con carne

1 Heat the oil in a frying pan and cook the onion and garlic until soft. Add the minced beef and cook until brown all over. Mix in the flour, salt to taste, chilli powder, tomatoes and beef stock. Stir the mixture well and bring to the boil. Reduce the heat and simmer gently for 30 minutes, stirring occasionally.

2 Drain the kidney beans, add to the chilli and cook for a further 5–10 minutes or until the kidney beans are heated through.

3 Serve the chilli immediately on a bed of boiled rice. Garnish with chopped parsley.

1 tablespoon oil

1 onion, chopped

2 garlic cloves, crushed

500 g (1 lb) minced beef

15 g (½ oz) plain flour

2 teaspoons chilli powder

400 g (13 oz) can tomatoes

300 ml (½ pint) beef stock

425 g (14 oz) can red kidney beans

salt

chopped parsley, to garnish

Serves 4

Preparation time: 10 minutes

Cooking time: 45 minutes

sausage waffles

1 Sift the flour, salt and baking powder into a bowl, adding any bran remaining in the sieve. In another bowl beat together the eggs, margarine and milk. Make a well in the centre of the flour and pour in half the egg and milk mixture. Beat together, drawing in the flour from the sides of the bowl. Gradually stir in the remaining liquid, beating hard to form a light, bubbly batter.

2 Lightly grease a waffle iron with oil and heat it on the hob, or use an electric waffle maker. Pour in just enough batter to cover the base of the iron. Close it and cook until golden. Remove the cooked waffle from the iron and keep it warm. Repeat with the remaining batter until it is all used up. Stack the waffles in layers with greaseproof paper between them.

3 Meanwhile, cook the sausages under a preheated grill, turning them frequently until evenly browned. Serve each waffle with 2 sausages and a spoonful of the tomato relish. Garnish with chopped chives.

250 g (8 oz) self-raising wholemeal flour

pinch of salt

1 teaspoon baking powder

2 eggs, beaten

75 g (3 oz) margarine, melted

450 ml (¾ pint) skimmed milk

soya or sunflower oil, for greasing

500 g (1 lb) low-fat pork sausages

tomato relish, to serve

chopped chives, to garnish

Serves 4
Preparation time: 30 minutes
Cooking time: 15–20 minutes

■ If you don't have a waffle maker, use a heavy frying pan instead, and make small pancakes with the batter.

1 Place 1 chicken breast at a time between 2 sheets of greaseproof paper and beat with a rolling pin or meat mallet to make a thin escalope, no more than 5 mm (¼ inch) thick.

2 Season the flour with salt and pepper and sprinkle on a plate. Beat together the egg and milk in a shallow dish.

3 Coat the escalopes in the seasoned flour, then dip into the egg and milk and coat with the breadcrumbs, pressing them on firmly with the palms of your hands.

4 Heat half of the butter and oil in a large frying pan. Add 2 of the escalopes and fry over a moderate heat for 4–5 minutes on each side, or until golden brown and cooked through. Keep warm while frying the remaining escalopes in the same way. Serve them at once, garnished with lemon wedges and watercress, accompanied by a mixed salad and sautéed potatoes.

4 boneless, skinless chicken breasts

1½ tablespoons plain flour

1 egg, beaten

1 tablespoon milk

125 g (4 oz) fresh white breadcrumbs

25 g (1 oz) butter

1 tablespoon vegetable oil

salt and pepper

To Garnish:

lemon wedges

watercress sprigs

Serves 4

Preparation time: 10 minutes

Cooking time: 15–20 minutes

chicken schnitzels

citrus chicken

1 Mix the garlic with the lemon and orange juice, add the cinnamon and season with salt and pepper. Pour into a shallow dish and add the chicken. Cover and leave to marinate for at least one hour.

2 Drain the chicken, reserving any marinade, and brush with oil. Cook on a greased grill rack under a preheated grill for about 10 minutes on each side. If any marinade is left, it can be heated and poured over the chicken before serving.

1 garlic clove, crushed

3 tablespoons lemon juice

4 tablespoons orange juice

pinch of ground cinnamon

4 chicken joints, skinned

oil, for brushing

salt and pepper

Serves 4

Preparation time: 15 minutes, plus marinating

Cooking time: 20 minutes

6 duck breasts, about 175 g (6 oz) each

salt

coriander sprigs, to garnish (optional)

Mango Relish:

1 tablespoon rapeseed oil

1 small onion, finely chopped

2.5 cm (1 inch) piece of fresh root ginger, peeled and crushed

1 garlic clove, crushed

3 ripe mangoes, diced

2 teaspoons dark brown sugar

¼ teaspoon cayenne pepper

2 tablespoons chopped fresh coriander

Serves 6
Preparation time: 30 minutes, plus chilling
Cooking time: 25 minutes

1 To make the mango relish, heat the oil in a pan, add the onion, ginger and garlic and fry gently, stirring for about 5 minutes until softened but not coloured. Add the mango, sugar, cayenne and a pinch of salt. Sauté for a few minutes or until the mango softens slightly. Remove from the heat, turn into a bowl and cool. Add the chopped coriander, cover and chill for at least 1 hour.

2 Score the duck breast skin in a criss-cross pattern with a very sharp knife then rub the skin with salt.

3 Put the duck skin-side up on a rack in a roasting tin. Place in a preheated oven, 200°C (400°F), Gas Mark 6, for 25 minutes, or until the duck is tender when pierced with a skewer or fork. When cooked remove from the rack and slice thinly on the diagonal. Serve with the mango relish and garnish with coriander sprigs if liked. Mangetout and new potatoes are ideal accompaniments.

■ Hot crispy duck with sweet and spicy mango relish makes an easy dish for entertaining. The relish can be made the day before, so all you have to do is roast the duck quickly in the oven before serving.

duck breasts with spicy mango relish

strawberry meringue baskets ●

peaches brûlée ●

cherry clafoutis ●

zabaglione ●

baked bananas with rum cream ●

papaya & pineapple flambé ●

double chocolate brownies ●

simple chocolate fudge ●

chocolate palmiers ●

chunky chocolate nut cookies ●

sweet
endings

strawberry meringue baskets

1 Spoon a little whipped cream into each meringue basket and arrange the whole strawberries on top. Brush the redcurrant jelly over the strawberries to glaze.

150 ml (¼ pint) double cream, whipped

8 ready-made meringue baskets

125 g (4 oz) strawberries

2 tablespoons redcurrant jelly, warmed

Serves 8

Preparation time: 10 minutes

6 fresh peaches, skinned

2 tablespoons Cointreau

300 ml (½ pint) double cream, whipped

125 g (4 oz) soft brown sugar

Serves 6
Preparation time: 10 minutes, plus cooling and chilling
Cooking time: 3 minutes

peaches brûlée

1 Halve the peaches, discard the stones and place the peaches cut-side up in a shallow ovenproof dish. Pour over the Cointreau.

2 Spoon the cream over the peaches to cover them completely and sprinkle with the sugar. Place under a preheated hot grill for 3 minutes or until the sugar has caramelized. Cool, then chill in the refrigerator before serving.

cherry clafoutis

1 Pit the cherries over a basin to make sure no juice is wasted.

2 Blend together the ingredients for the batter in a mixing bowl. Grease a 1.5–1.8 litre (2½–3 pint) pie or soufflé dish with the butter. Heat for a few minutes then add the pitted cherries and any juice. Cover with the batter.

3 Bake the pudding in a preheated oven, 200°C (400°F), Gas Mark 6, for 30 minutes or until well risen. Sift icing sugar lightly over the top and serve at once.

500 g (1 lb) ripe black cherries

15 g (½ oz) butter

icing sugar, for dusting

Batter:

75 g (3 oz) plain flour

25 g (1 oz) caster sugar

3 large eggs

225 ml (7½ fl oz) milk

few drops of vanilla essence

Serves 4
Preparation time: 15 minutes
Cooking time: 30–35 minutes

zabaglione

1 Place the egg yolks in the top of a double boiler, or in a bowl sitting over a small saucepan of gently simmering water. Make sure that the bowl is not in contact with the water.

2 Add the sugar and Marsala or sweet white wine to the egg yolks and stir well. Beat the mixture with either a wire whisk or a hand-held electric whisk until the zabaglione is thick, light and hot. Even with an electric whisk, this will take 10–15 minutes, so be patient. Check that the water simmers gently underneath and that the pan does not boil dry.

3 When the zabaglione is cooked, pour it carefully into 4 tall glasses and serve immediately.

4 Alternatively, to serve the zabaglione cold, continue beating the mixture off the heat, until it has cooled down completely. Mix the cold zabaglione with raspberries, sliced strawberries or peaches, if liked.

4 egg yolks

5 tablespoons sugar

8 tablespoons Marsala or sweet white wine

Serves 4

Preparation time: 2–3 minutes

Cooking time: 10–15 minutes

baked bananas with rum cream

1 Mix the sugar, cinnamon and rum in a bowl. Stir in the mascarpone, mix well and set aside.

2 Place the whole unpeeled bananas on a barbecue grill over hot coals or under a preheated grill. Cook for 10–12 minutes, turning the bananas as the skins darken, until they are black all over and the flesh is very tender.

3 To serve, split the bananas open and spread the flesh with the rum mascarpone cream.

1–2 tablespoons caster sugar

½ teaspoon ground cinnamon

2 teaspoons rum

250 g (8 oz) mascarpone cheese

8 small bananas

Serves 4
Preparation time: 5 minutes
Cooking time: 10–12 minutes

■ Mascarpone is a rich Italian cream cheese, sold in plastic tubs in many delicatessens and supermarkets. In this recipe it could be replaced by another Italian cheese, ricotta.

papaya & pineapple flambé

1 Peel the papayas and scoop out the seeds. Cut the flesh into slices. Peel the pineapple and cut it into thin slices. Remove the central core so you are left with pineapple rings.

2 Melt the butter in a large heavy-based frying pan, then stir in the sugar over a low heat, stirring until it has thoroughly dissolved. Add the lime juice and grated rind.

3 Increase the heat slightly and let the sugary mixture bubble for a few minutes until thickened. Take care that it does not burn or turn to caramel. Add the papaya and pineapple and cook gently for 2 minutes. Sprinkle the mixture with ground cinnamon.

4 Add the tequila to the pan, then stand well back and set it alight, using a long taper. When the flames die down, divide the flambéed papaya and pineapple among 4 individual serving dishes. Decorate each one with slivers of lime rind and serve with a bowl of crème fraîche.

2 papayas

1 small pineapple

50 g (2 oz) butter

50 g (2 oz) soft brown sugar

juice and grated rind of 1 lime

½ teaspoon ground cinnamon

4 tablespoons tequila

slivers of lime rind, to decorate

crème fraîche, to serve

Serves 4
Preparation time: 10 minutes
Cooking time: 10 minutes

■ Papaya, or pawpaw, is a large pear-shaped tropical fruit. The skin is yellowish, while its flesh is salmon pink with dark seeds in the central cavity. It has a fairly sweet taste and is often served with a squeeze of lemon or lime to bring out its full flavour.

double chocolate brownies

1 Grease and line a 28 x 20 cm (11 x 8 inch) shallow baking tin with greaseproof paper. Break up 125 g (4 oz) of the white chocolate and put in a heatproof bowl with the butter. Leave over a saucepan of simmering water until melted. Stir lightly. Roughly chop the remaining white chocolate and the plain chocolate.

2 Whisk the eggs and sugar together in a large bowl until foamy. Beat in the melted chocolate mixture. Sift the flour into the bowl and stir it into the mixture with the almond essence, walnuts and chopped white and plain chocolate.

3 Turn the brownie mixture into the prepared tin and bake in a preheated oven, 190°C (375°F), Gas Mark 5, for 35 minutes until risen and just firm. Leave the baked mixture in the tin to cool.

4 When cool, turn out of the tin on to a board and cut into squares and rectangles.

375 g (12 oz) white chocolate

50 g (2 oz) unsalted butter

250 g (8 oz) plain chocolate

3 eggs

150 g (5 oz) caster sugar

175 g (6 oz) self-raising flour

1 teaspoon almond essence

150 g (5 oz) broken walnuts

Makes 14–16

Preparation time: 20 minutes, plus cooling

Cooking time: 35 minutes

simple chocolate fudge

1 Grease and line the base and halfway up the sides of an 18 cm (7 inch) square cake tin with nonstick greaseproof paper.

2 Put the sugar in a large heavy-based saucepan with the milk, butter and vanilla essence, and heat gently until the sugar dissolves. Bring to the boil and boil for 5–10 minutes, stirring frequently, until the temperature reaches 115°C (240°F) on a sugar thermometer. (Alternatively, drop a teaspoon of the mixture into a bowl of iced water. You should then be able to roll the mixture into a ball between your fingers.)

3 Remove the pan from the heat and beat in the plain chocolate until melted. Pour into the prepared tin and leave for several hours until set.

4 Remove the fudge from the tin and peel away the paper. Cut the fudge into small squares. Leave on a greaseproof paper-lined tray to dry out. The fudge will keep in an airtight container or jar for up to 2 weeks.

250 g (8 oz) sugar

425 g (14 oz) can sweetened condensed milk

25 g (1 oz) unsalted butter

1 teaspoon vanilla essence

250 g (8 oz) plain chocolate, broken into pieces

Makes 50–60 pieces

Preparation time: 20 minutes, plus setting and drying

Cooking time: 10–15 minutes

■ If you like you can decorate the fudge with chocolate. Put 125 g (4 oz) plain or milk chocolate, broken into pieces, in a heatproof bowl over a saucepan of simmering water and leave until melted. Holding a piece of fudge between forefinger and thumb, dip it into the chocolate to coat the base and 3 mm ($^1/_8$ inch) up the sides. Return to the greaseproof paper and leave to set.

1 Mix the grated chocolate with half of the caster sugar.

2 Roll out the puff pastry on a lightly floured surface to a 20 cm (8 inch) square and sprinkle with the remaining caster sugar. Continue rolling the pastry until the square measures about 28 cm (11 inches) across. Brush with beaten egg and sprinkle with the chocolate and sugar mixture.

3 Roll up the pastry from one side until you reach the centre, then roll up the other side so the 2 rolls meet in the middle of the square. Brush the points where the rolls meet with a little beaten egg.

4 Using a sharp knife, cut across the rolls to make about 24 thin slices. Roll the slices very lightly to flatten and place on lightly greased baking sheets. Bake in a preheated oven, 220°C (425°F), Gas Mark 7, for about 10 minutes, until golden. Transfer to a wire rack to cool. Sprinkle with caster sugar to serve.

25 g (1 oz) plain chocolate, grated

50 g (2 oz) caster sugar

250 g (8 oz) puff pastry

beaten egg, to glaze

caster sugar, to serve

Makes about 24

Preparation time: 10–15 minutes, plus cooling

Cooking time: 10 minutes

chocolate palmiers

chunky chocolate nut cookies

1 Beat the butter and sugar together in a bowl until pale and creamy. Add the egg, flour, baking powder and porridge oats, and beat until well combined.

2 Stir in the chocolate and peanuts and mix well. Using a dessertspoon, place spoonfuls of the mixture, spaced slightly apart, on greased baking sheets. Flatten slightly with a fork. Bake in a preheated oven, 180°C (350°F), Gas Mark 4, for 15–20 minutes.

3 Leave the cookies on the baking sheets for 2 minutes, then transfer to a wire rack to cool. Serve dusted with icing sugar, if liked.

125 g (4 oz) lightly salted butter, softened

125 g (4 oz) light muscovado sugar

1 egg, lightly beaten

150 g (5 oz) plain flour, sifted

½ teaspoon baking powder

75 g (3 oz) porridge oats

200 g (7 oz) plain chocolate, roughly chopped

50 g (2 oz) unsalted peanuts, roughly chopped

icing sugar, for dusting (optional)

Makes 28
Preparation time: 20 minutes, plus cooling
Cooking time: 15–20 minutes

index

apple & Stilton pork 72
avocado & prawn mayo sandwiches 36

bananas baked with rum cream 89
bean sprouts: chow mein 41
beef: beef & mushroom burgers 69
  beef kebabs with horseradish salsa 68
  beef with mushrooms 44
  chilli con carne 76
  green pepper steak 74
  steak au poivre 75
beetroot: beetroot & pink grapefruit salad 22
  rosy beetroot salad 23
bread, stuffed French 16

carrot & ginger soup 33
cheese: croque monsieur 14
  Greek salad 27
  pear & Stilton salad 19
  Reuben sandwich 12
  two-tomato & mozzarella salad 24
cherry clafoutis 87
chicken: chicken schnitzels 78
  citrus chicken 79
chilli con carne 76
chocolate: chocolate palmiers 94
  chunky chocolate nut cookies 95
  double chocolate brownies 91
  simple chocolate fudge 92
chow mein 41
cod: cod kebabs with barbecue sauce 57
  cod steaks à la grecque 56
  fish casserole with peppers 64
  fishy baked spuds 59
  spicy fried fishcakes 61
  spinach & cod omelette 58
crab bisque 31
croque monsieur 14
curry, Thai vegetable 47

duck breasts with spicy mango relish 80

eggs: spinach & cod omelette 58
  vegetable frittata 48

fishcakes, spicy fried 61
focaccia pizzas with pepperoni 17
French bread, stuffed 16
frittata, vegetable 48

grapefruit: beetroot & pink grapefruit salad 22
Greek salad 27
green pepper steak 74

haddock fritters, spicy 60
ham: Mediterranean spaghetti with 53
  quick pizza with cheese & 49
hot & sour Thai noodles 40

lamb with cranberries & honey 71

Mediterranean spaghetti with ham 53
melon salad, summer 20

meringue baskets, strawberry 84
mushrooms: beef & mushroom burgers 69
  beef with mushrooms 44
  mushroom soup 34

nectarine & avocado salad, Tuscan 21
noodles: chow mein 41
  hot & sour Thai noodles 40

papaya & pineapple flambé 90
pasta with mixed seafood sauce 50
pasta with tuna & mushrooms 52
pâté, prawn & soft cheese 37
peaches brûlée 85
pear & Stilton salad 19
peppers, fish casserole with 64
pineapple: papaya & pineapple flambé 90
pizzas 17, 49
pork: apple & Stilton pork 72
  pork chops with cider 73
potatoes: fishy baked spuds 59
  hot potato salad 28
prawns: avocado & prawn mayo sandwiches 36
  fishy baked spuds 59
  prawn & soft cheese pâté 37
  prawn chilli fry 62
  stir-fried prawn supper 45

red kidney beans: chilli con carne 76
Reuben sandwich 12

salade Niçoise 26
salads 19–29
salami, mozzarella & pepper toasts 15
salmon steaks in red wine 65
sandwiches 12, 36
sausage waffles 77
seafood sauce, pasta with 50
soups 31–4
spaghetti with ham, Mediterranean 53
spinach & cod omelette 58
steak au poivre 75
strawberry meringue baskets 84

Thai vegetable curry 47
tomatoes: creamy tomato soup 32
  two-tomato & mozzarella salad 24
tuna, pasta with mushrooms & 52
turkey: stir-fried with pine nuts & green
peppers 43
  turkey & orange stir-fry 46
  warm turkey salad 29
Tuscan nectarine & avocado salad 21

vegetable frittata 48

zabaglione 88